To Ed and Magie Li,
for taking care of our zoo
when we're away — K. K.

To Hyemi — M. H.

TEXT COPYRIGHT © 2014 BY KATHLEEN KRULL
ILLUSTRATIONS COPYRIGHT © 2014 BY MARCELLUS HALL

ALL RIGHTS RESERVED. PUBLISHED BY ARTHUR A. LEVINE BOOKS, AN IMPRINT OF SCHOLASTIC INC., *PUBLISHERS SINCE 1920.*
SCHOLASTIC AND THE LANTERN LOGO ARE TRADEMARKS AND/OR REGISTERED TRADEMARKS OF SCHOLASTIC INC.

NO PART OF THIS PUBLICATION MAY BE REPRODUCED, STORED IN A RETRIEVAL SYSTEM, OR TRANSMITTED IN ANY FORM OR
BY ANY MEANS, ELECTRONIC, MECHANICAL, PHOTOCOPYING, RECORDING, OR OTHERWISE, WITHOUT WRITTEN PERMISSION
OF THE PUBLISHER. FOR INFORMATION REGARDING PERMISSION, WRITE TO SCHOLASTIC INC.,
ATTENTION: PERMISSIONS DEPARTMENT, 557 BROADWAY, NEW YORK, NY 10012.

LIBRARY OF CONGRESS CATALOGING-IN-PUBLICATION DATA

KRULL, KATHLEEN.
WHAT'S NEW? THE ZOO!: A ZIPPY HISTORY OF ZOOS / BY KATHLEEN KRULL;
ILLUSTRATED BY MARCELLUS HALL. — FIRST EDITION.
PAGES CM
INCLUDES BIBLIOGRAPHICAL REFERENCES.
ISBN 978-0-545-13571-9 (ALK. PAPER)
1. ZOOS — HISTORY. I. HALL, MARCELLUS, ILLUSTRATOR. II. TITLE.
III. TITLE: WHAT'S NEW? THE ZOO! IV. TITLE: ZIPPY HISTORY OF ZOOS.

QL76.H338 2014   590.73 — DC23   2013021189

10 9 8 7 6 5 4 3 2 1   14 15 16 17 18

PRINTED IN MALAYSIA   108
FIRST EDITION, JULY 2014

THE TEXT WAS SET IN 12-POINT BOOK ANTIQUA.
THE DISPLAY WAS SET IN CIRCUSMOUSE AND BERNARD MT CONDENSED.
THE ILLUSTRATIONS WERE CREATED USING CALLIACRYLIC INK AND WATERCOLOR PAINT ON WATERCOLOR PAPER.
BOOK DESIGN BY MARIJKA KOSTIW

Are you ready for a trip to the zoo?

You might think that zoos are new, but they've been around for thousands of years.

That's right — we have always loved to look at elephants, giraffes, gorillas, lions, and so much more.

4,400 YEARS AGO, THE SUMERIAN CITY OF UR, IN PRESENT-DAY IRAQ

The king of beasts lunges and roars. The King of Ur roars right back, feeling like the ruler of all nature. How delicious to wield his power over dangerous animals! It's the world's first known zoo, and all we're sure about (from clay tablets in libraries) is that it has lions.

**3,500 YEARS AGO,
IN PRESENT-DAY ETHIOPIA**

Queens prize wild animals,
too. Egyptian Pharaoh-Queen
Hatshepsut already has a lifetime
supply of gold, so she sends ships
down the African coast to trade for
what will make her appear even mightier —
expensive leopards, cheetahs, greyhounds,
exotic birds, and a most mysterious giraffe.

3,000 YEARS AGO, CHINA

Can animals make you smarter?
Yes, says Emperor Wen-Wang,
deeming his vast zoo "The
Garden of Intelligence." Full of
yaks, turtles, goats, alligators, and
possibly giant pandas, this is where he
contemplates nature. Animals are believed to
go back and forth between the human and spirit
worlds, so it's a sacred space.

2,400 YEARS AGO, GREECE

The Greeks leap ahead in understanding animals, learning how they differ from each other, how they reproduce. Wise Aristotle, the scholarly son of the royal doctor, spends endless hours in his private zoo. He studies monkeys, talking parrots, and so many other creatures that he's able to write *The History of Animals*, our first encyclopedia about them.

2,300 YEARS AGO, ALEXANDRIA, EGYPT

Named for Aristotle's most famous pupil, world conqueror Alexander the Great, the grand city of Alexandria has a library to end all libraries, and a zoo to end all zoos. When the animals stroll past its stadium, it takes an entire day — ninety-six elephants, sixty wild goats, three hundred exotic sheep, twenty-four lions, sixteen ostriches, a python over thirty feet long, and thousands of dogs, oxen, and oryxes.

ABOUT 30 BC, OUTSIDE ROME, ITALY

Rich Romans cocoon themselves in their country villas with the best of all status symbols — private zoos. One scholar named Marcus Terentius Varro has a zest for birds, building a domed hall with separate aviaries for talking starlings, songbirds, and peafowl. At lavish dinners, lucky guests sit in the center of the hall and listen while they eat.

ABOUT 790 AD, FRANCE AND GERMANY

With the fall of the Roman Empire, hundred of years pass with little news for
zoos. Then Emperor Charlemagne starts collecting animals from other rulers.
The caliph of Baghdad sends him a big surprise — an elephant. How many royal
zoos does it take to show Charlemagne's greatness? Three. And his animals live
in better conditions than most people.

1271, CHINA

Kublai Khan wants to prove he's no mere Mongolian warrior, so he collects tigers, boars, lynx, porcupines, falcons, civets, and deer — animals worthy of his new status as the emperor of China. He keeps ten thousand white horses at his Xanadu summer palace, as he adores their milk.

1513, ROME, ITALY

Pope Leo X tends a nice little zoo, to which smart rulers send gifts. One day, Hanno the elephant arrives from the Portuguese king. She disobeys the order to kneel. Instead, she dips her trunk in a fountain of holy water and sprays everyone, including the pope.

THE 1500s, PRESENT-DAY MEXICO CITY

Aztec emperor Moctezuma II spares no expense in housing his pumas, jaguars, sloths, armadillos, llamas, poisonous snakes with bells attached to their tails, and birds (a whole palace just for them). It takes six hundred men and women, in addition to a staff of nurses, to care for the largest zoo of its time and one of the largest in world history.

ABOUT 1580, AFGHANISTAN AND INDIA

Akbar the Great treats his one thousand cheetahs more kindly than most people of his time. To care for them and the other animals he befriends, he builds zoos much grander than any in Europe in the lands he conquers. At the entrance to each zoo, he posts some advice: "Meet your brothers. Take them to your hearts and respect them."

1735, SWEDEN

Thanks to new trade routes with the Americas and Asia, European zoo collections grow much more diverse. At the Swedish royal family's zoo, a scientist named Carl Linnaeus classifies animals into species with his *System of Nature*. The book gives a jolt of energy to the Scientific Revolution by establishing a whole new branch of science — zoology, which deals with animals.

1749, VERSAILLES, FRANCE

The people of France crave traveling spectacles, and Clara, the most famous rhinoceros in history, journeys all the way from India to spend five months wowing them. She stands six feet high and about twelve feet around, and she weighs six thousand pounds — but King Louis XV lets Clara nibble roses from his own royal hand.

1827, PARIS, FRANCE

"So that's what a giraffe looks like!" say the French upon glimpsing the new gift from an Egyptian ruler to King Charles X. The giraffe takes a sensational three-day walk from the docks in Marseilles to her new home at the Jardin des Plantes zoo. Wearing a waterproof cape, she steps through fields of sunflowers, pine forests, orchards, and vineyards, accompanied by three cows that provide her milk. She inspires songs, poems, paintings, products of all kinds, and even a tall new hairdo, *à la Girafe*.

1835, LONDON, ENGLAND

The Industrial Revolution erects tall buildings and ugly factories, making people long to get back to nature. They escape to the world's first modern zoo — open only to scientists at first, but then, in 1846, to anyone who can afford the penny fee. Ordinary families flock to see Tommy Chimpanzee, who took the night coach in from Bristol on the last leg of his journey from Africa. "The folks in town are nearly wild / To go and see the monkey child," declares a popular poem.

1838, LONDON, ENGLAND

Jenny the orangutan is even more spellbinding. Who is that man studying her as he plays harmonica, gives her a mirror, and lets her taste a peppermint? It's Charles Darwin, about to become famous for his new ideas in biology. Jenny acts "precisely like a naughty child," he observes.

1865, LONDON, ENGLAND

Jumbo the elephant is gigantically popular, as well as just gigantic. He gorges on vast amounts of whiskey, onions, apples, and cakes, and grows to weigh six and a half tons. Years later, when American P. T. Barnum buys him for his new circus, a hundred thousand children write to Queen Victoria, begging her to stop the sale.

1862, MELBOURNE, AUSTRALIA

Somehow, a city no longer seems like a proper
city unless it has a public zoo for amusement
and entertainment. When the city of Melbourne
is only twenty-seven years old, it starts up a
zoo, advertising for anyone coming to Australia
to bring animals to it. But it's the local creatures
that draw the crowds: kangaroos, emus, koalas,
wallabies, and hairy-nosed wombats.

1875, KOLKATA, INDIA

The Alipore Zoological Garden in Kolkata opens with donations from private animal collections. It has gazelles, antelope, and a snake lab for testing antidotes to poisonous venom. But after many years, certain animals become hard to find. To help with this problem, this zoo is one of the first to breed white tigers, not to mention short-spined porcupines, agoutis, mongooses, and lemurs. Indian leader Mahatma Gandhi later declares, "The greatness of a nation . . . can be judged by the way its animals are treated."

1889, WASHINGTON, DC

The United States' National Zoo becomes the first to proclaim a goal of protecting "those native animals that were threatened with extinction" so that they "might live and perpetuate their species in peace." But money is limited in its early years, so the zoo depends on donations of raccoons, possums, and other not-very-rare animals that people no longer want.

1898, SOUTH AFRICA

Black and white rhinos, so very scarce elsewhere, still thrive here, because South African president Paul Kruger creates a reserve to protect them. A century later, Kruger National Park will have too many rhinos and will send hundreds to live in zoos elsewhere.

1907, NEAR HAMBURG, GERMANY

Carl Hagenbeck has long bought and exhibited animals, but now he has a new idea for an "animal paradise." Wild animals are no longer inhumanely locked away; instead, they're separated from people by clever moats, artificial rocks, trees, and hedges.

Eingang

Ecstatic viewers have the illusion of gazing at panoramas of Africa, with deer grazing, flamingos flapping, antelopes and zebras playing, a cliff for vultures, and wild goats in the distance. Zoos around the world rush to imitate the first zoo without cages.

1907, NEW YORK, NEW YORK

Fifteen very confused American buffalo stick out in the crowd at Grand Central Terminal. They've come from the Bronx Zoo to board a train to Oklahoma as part

of a program to prevent buffalo from disappearing in the West. It's a turning point in zoo history — the first time that endangered animals are reintroduced into their original home — and it works.

1964, TOKYO, JAPAN

Shimmering goldfish and jellyfish calm visitors to Japan's oldest zoological complex,

the Ueno Zoo. One thousand gorgeous cherry trees surround its wild ducks, penguins, Komodo dragons, and Japanese cranes with their red crowns.

1978, SEATTLE, WASHINGTON

Kiki and the other gorillas at Woodland Park Zoo climb into their new home, uniquely dense with real plants and trees. Some visitors complain that the zoo is so lush they can't see the animals. But like many zoos now, this one displays animals not for show, but for scientists to learn how gorillas act in their natural habitat. These gorillas become so playful and peaceful that they give scientists new ideas about what gorillas are really like.

1981, OUTSIDE RIO DE JANEIRO, BRAZIL

Brazilian scientists, working with the
United States' National Zoo, begin a program
to rescue golden lion tamarins from extinction. In
two years, the number of these velvety little monkeys
in captivity explodes from eighty to three hundred
seventy. Then scientists begin reintroducing
them into forests. The goal is to reach two
thousand in the wild by 2025.

1995, BALI, INDONESIA

More and more, zoos are places that protect animals. One of the rarest species of all, the tiny Bali starling, thrives here at Bali Bird Park. This sanctuary shelters rare birds from Indonesia, Latin America, and South Africa, including birds of paradise, serpent eagles, and the hyacinth macaw, the largest parrot in the world.

2009, SAN DIEGO, CALIFORNIA

Yun Zi, or "Son of Cloud," is born under cloudless skies at the San Diego Zoo — the fifth rare panda born here. He starts munching bamboo and will become a cuddly-looking giant — one of the most popular animals ever.

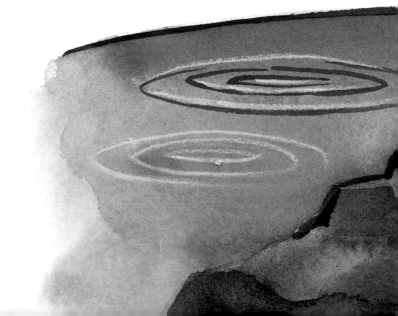

All throughout history, zoos have been built for so many reasons.

To make important people feel more important.

To satisfy our longing for contact with nature.

To educate, amuse, and entertain.

To make us gasp with awe.

To study and protect animals.

Whatever your reason, visit a zoo today.

Listen to the lions roar!

SOURCES

Alipore Zoological Garden, www.kolkatazoo.in

Allin, Michael. *Zarafa: A Giraffe's True Story, from Deep in Africa to the Heart of Paris.* NY: Walker & Company, 1998.

Association of Zoos & Aquariums, www.aza.org

Arizona-Sonora Desert Museum, www.desertmuseum.org

Bali Bird Park, www.bali-bird-park.com

Bell, Catharine E., ed. *Encyclopedia of the World's Zoos.* Chicago: Fitzroy Dearborn Publishers, 2001.

Bonner, Jeffrey P. *Sailing with Noah: Stories from the World of Zoos.* Columbia: University of Missouri Press, 2006.

Bronx Zoo, www.bronxzoo.com

Croke, Vicki. *The Modern Ark: The Story of Zoos: Past, Present and Future.* NY: Avon Books, 1998.

Hancocks, David. *A Different Nature: The Paradoxical World of Zoos and Their Uncertain Future.* Berkeley: University of California Press, 2001.

Hoage, R. J. and William A. Deiss, ed. *New Worlds, New Animals: From Menagerie to Zoological Park in the Nineteenth Century.* Baltimore: Johns Hopkins University Press, 1996.

Kisling, Vernon N., Jr., ed. *Zoo and Aquarium History: Ancient Animal Collections to Zoological Gardens.* Boca Raton, FL: CRC Press, 2001.

Kruger National Park, www.krugerpark.co.za

London Zoo, www.zsl.org/zsl-london-zoo

Melbourne Zoo, www.zoo.org.au/Melbourne

National Zoo, nationalzoo.si.edu/default.cfm

Ridley, Glynis. *Clara's Grand Tour: Travels with a Rhinoceros in Eighteenth-Century Europe.* NY: Atlantic Monthly Press, 2004.

Rothfels, Nigel. *Savages and Beasts: The Birth of the Modern Zoo.* Baltimore: Johns Hopkins University Press, 2002.

St. Louis Zoo, www.stlzoo.org

San Diego Zoo Giant Panda Research Station, www.sandiegozoo.org/pandacam

Tierpark Hagenbeck, www.hagenbeck.de/en/tierpark/start.html

Ueno Zoo, www.tokyo-zoo.net/english/ueno/main.html

Woodland Park Zoo, Seattle, www.zoo.org

World Association of Zoos and Aquariums, www.waza.org

Zoehfeld, Kathleen Weidner. *Wild Lives: A History of the People and Animals of the Bronx Zoo.* NY: Knopf, 2006.

ZooBorns, www.zooborns.com

Zoos Worldwide, www.zoos-worldwide.de